CLASSIC PIANO REPERTOIRE

JOHN THOMPSON

9 GREAT PIANO SOLOS

ISBN 978-1-4768-8957-3

WILLIS MUSIC

EXCLUSIVELY DISTRIBUTED BY

HAL•LEONARD®
CORPORATION

7777 W. BLUEMOUND RD. P.O. BOX 13819 MILWAUKEE, WI 53213

Visit Hal Leonard Online at
www.halleonard.com

"I think I first knew I was going to be interested in music when I learned my first piece in the **JOHN THOMPSON** book. Everybody who's ever taken piano lessons has to take a John Thompson course."

— Billy Joel, American pianist and singer-songwriter,
in a 1980 interview with Tom Hoving on ABC's *20/20*

"I grew up learning **JOHN THOMPSON's** pieces. I loved them then, and I love them still – I could not have asked for a better beginning! Basic concepts were soundly introduced, but in the most charming way so that I was always eager for more. The wonderful thing about Thompson's pieces is that they teach the crucial pianistic skills, so progress is assured."

— Dr. Peter Mack, professor of piano at Cornish College
January 2013

JOHN THOMPSON (1889-1963) was born in Williamstown, Pennsylvania, the eldest of four children of James and Emma Thompson. He began music study at the age of five, and his parents encouraged his prodigious talent by sending him to study piano with Maurits Leefson at the Leefson-Hille Conservatory in Philadelphia, graduating in 1909. At the same time, he studied composition with Dr. Hugh Clark at the University of Pennsylvania. In his early twenties Thompson toured the United States and Europe as a concert pianist, receiving respectable reviews and performing with several European orchestras. He was in London when the start of World War I abruptly ended his concert career. After his return to the United States, he began a distinguished career as a pedagogue, heading music conservatories in Indianapolis, Philadelphia, as well as the Kansas City Conservatory of Music (now University of Missouri at Kansas City). It was during these tenures that he developed his distinctive ideas about teaching young children and adults and began his prolific composing and publishing career.

His best-selling method books *Teaching Little Fingers to Play* and *Modern Course for the Piano* were first published by the Willis Music Company in the mid-1930s and soon grew to include the *Easiest Piano Course* and other notable educational publications. These publications have had a profound influence on millions of musicians today, and continue to have an impact on the teaching of piano in America and throughout the world.

FROM THE PUBLISHERS

The *Classic Piano Repertoire* series includes popular as well as lesser-known pieces from a select group of composers out of the Willis piano archives (established in 1899). This volume features nine original piano solos by John Thompson ranging from early to later elementary. Each piece has been newly engraved and edited with the aim to preserve Thompson's primary intent and musical purpose.

Of special interest is the fact that several Thompson pieces were initially published under pseudonyms. For the purpose of this book, every piece is properly credited to Thompson.

CONTENTS

John Thompson, age 28.

Toy Ships

John Thompson

Moderato

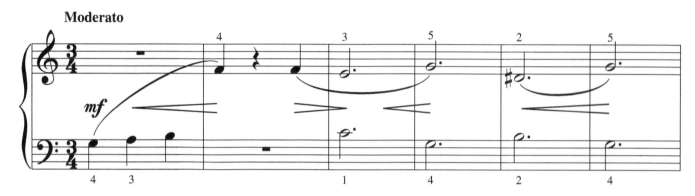

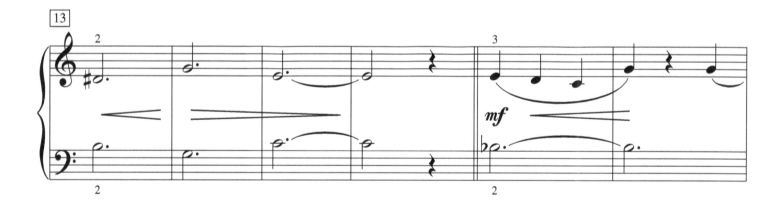

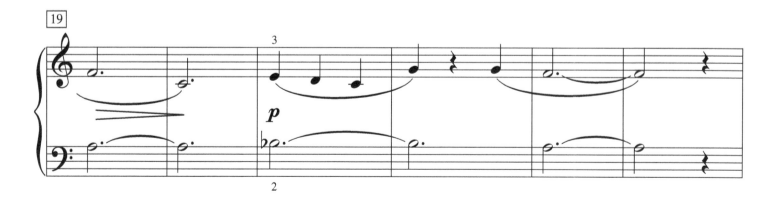

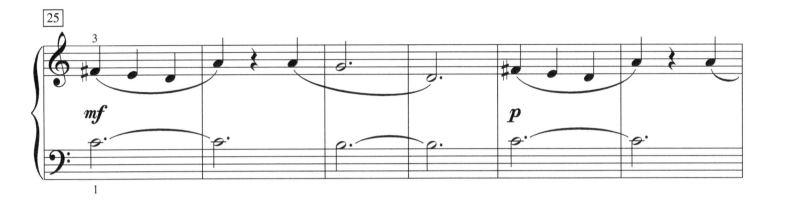

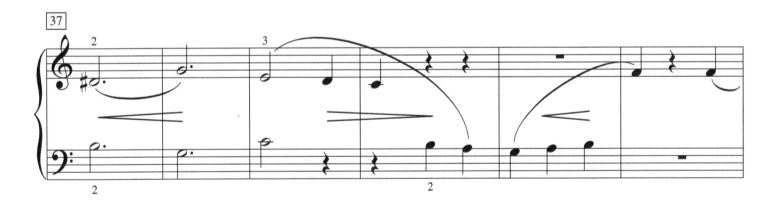

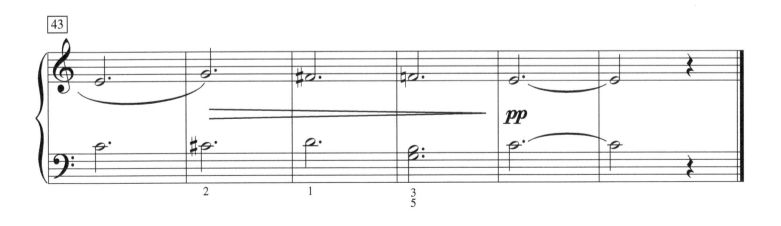

Forest Dawn

John Thompson

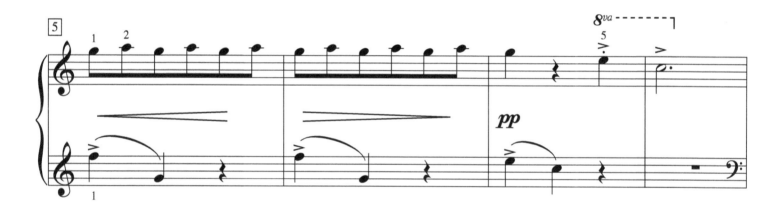

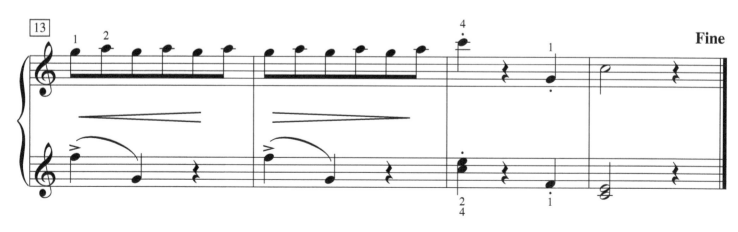

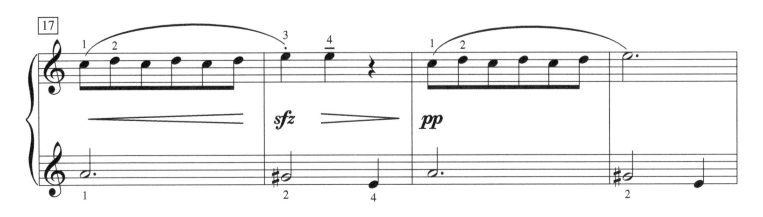

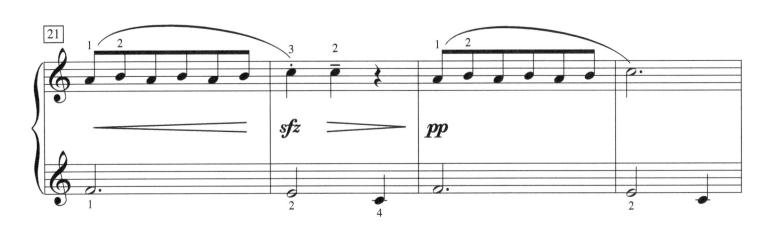

D.C. al Fine

Dutch Dance

John Thompson

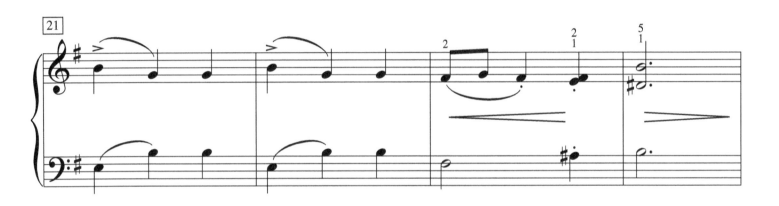

D.C. al Fine

Southern Shuffle

John Thompson

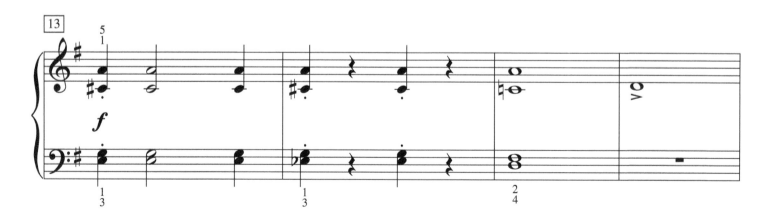

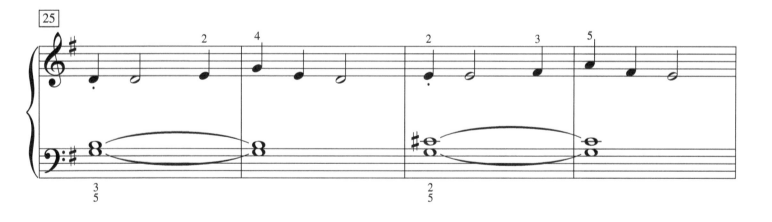

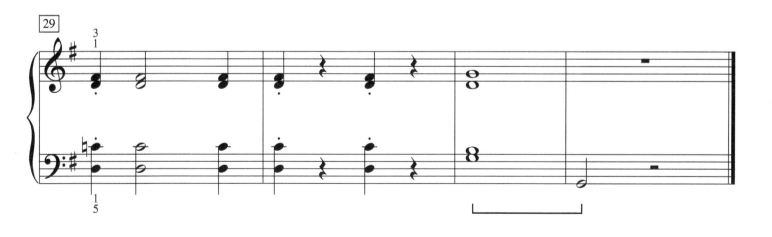

Captain Kidd

John Thompson

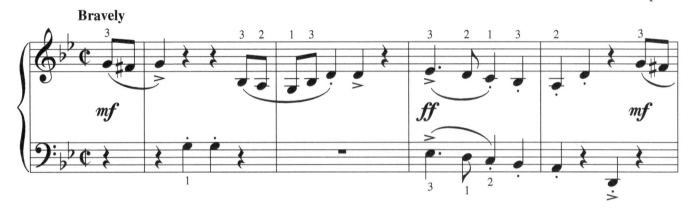

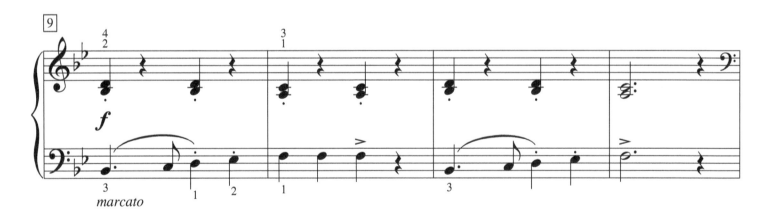

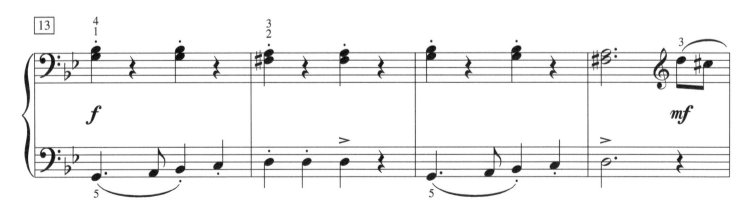

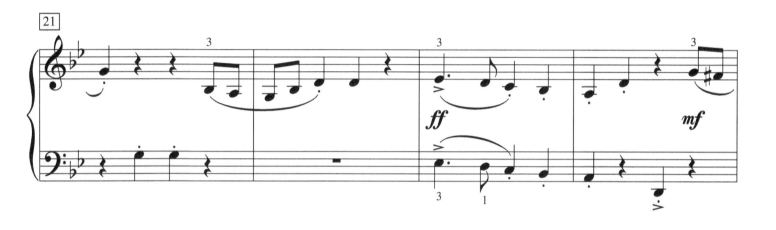

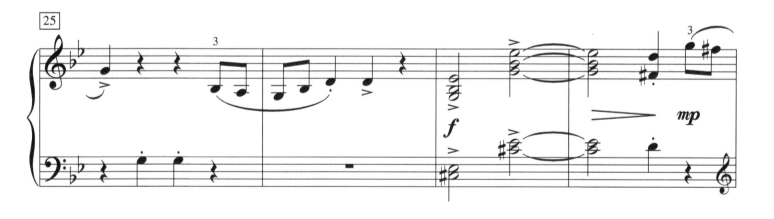

Up in the Air

Up in the air midst fleecy clouds
And sharp winds, swinging high;
The pilot is like an eagle bold
Oh! but it's great to fly!

John Thompson

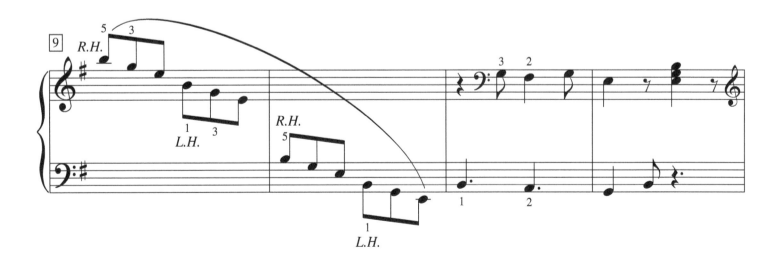

Tiptoe

John Thompson

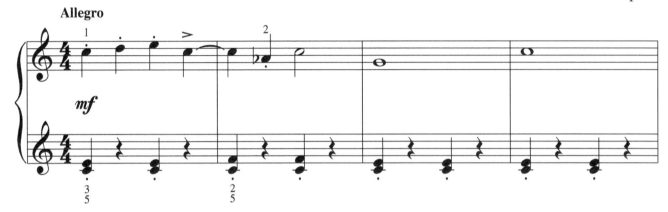

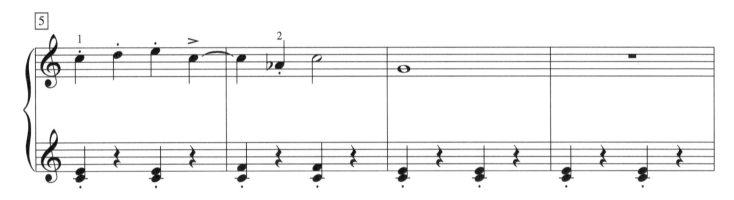

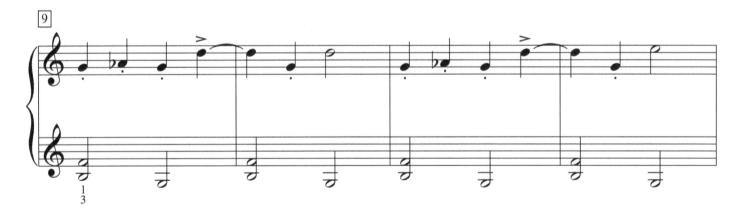

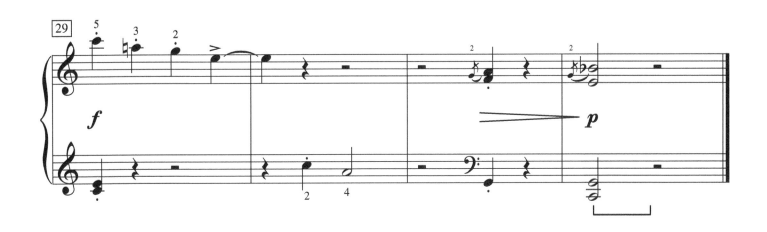

Drowsy Moon

John Thompson

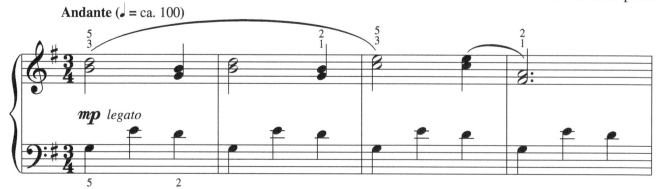

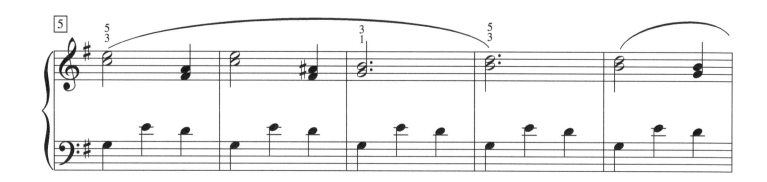

2nd Time to Coda ⊕

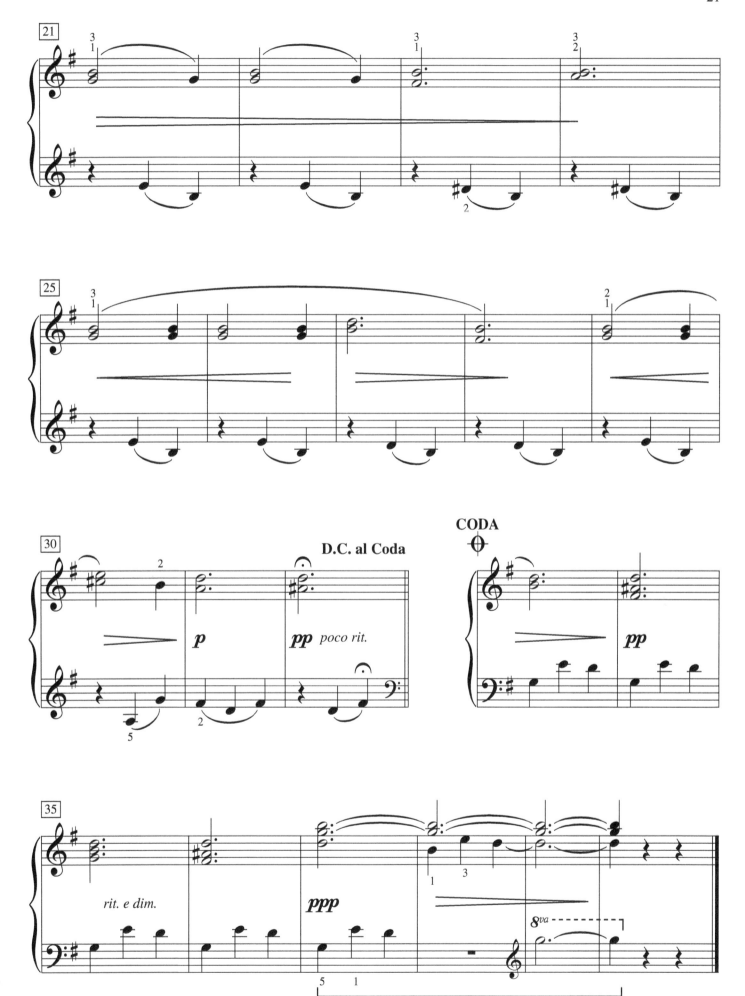

Humoresque

John Thompson

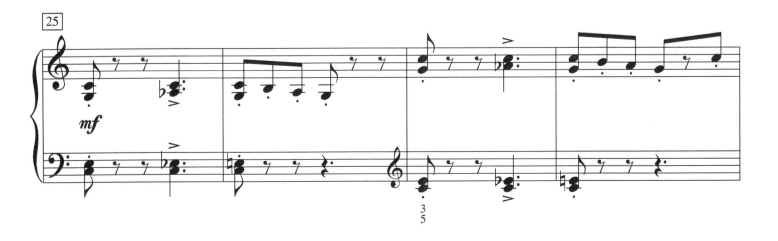